GETTING TO KNOW
THE U.S. PRESIDENTS

A N D R E W
JACKSON

SEVENTH PRESIDENT
1829 – 1837

WRITTEN AND ILLUSTRATED BY MIKE VENEZIA

CHILDREN'S PRESS®
A DIVISION OF SCHOLASTIC INC.
NEW YORK   TORONTO   LONDON   AUCKLAND   SYDNEY
MEXICO CITY   NEW DELHI   HONG KONG
DANBURY, CONNECTICUT

Reading Consultant: Nanci R. Vargus, Ed.D., Assistant Professor, School of Education, University of Indianapolis

Historical Consultant: Marc J. Selverstone, Ph.D., Assistant Professor, Miller Center of Public Affairs, University of Virginia

Photographs © 2005: Art Resource, NY/National Portrait Gallery, Smithsonian Institution: 3; Corbis Images/Bettmann: 19 left, 24, 26; Getty Images/MPI: 11; Hulton Archive/Getty Images: 25; Library of Congress: 32 (via SODA), 22; North Wind Picture Archives: 5; Old Salem Inc./Collection of the Wachovia Historical Society: 4; Stock Montage, Inc.: 27; Superstock, Inc.: 8, 19 right, 20; The Hermitage: Home of President Andrew Jackson, Nashville, TN: 9, 10, 14, 23; The Philbrook Museum of Art, Tulsa, Oklahoma: 28, 29 (Choctaw Removal, 1966, Valjean McCarty Hessing, Choctaw, b. 1934, watercolor on paper, Museum purchase, 1967.24).

Colorist for illustrations: Dave Ludwig

Library of Congress Cataloging-in-Publication Data

Venezia, Mike.
  Andrew Jackson / written and illustrated by Mike Venezia.
      p. cm. — (Getting to know the U.S. presidents)
  Includes bibliographical references and index.
  ISBN 0-516-22612-6 (lib. bdg.)   0-516-27481-3 (pbk.)
  1. Jackson, Andrew, 1767-1845—Juvenile literature. 2. Presidents—United
States—Biography—Juvenile literature. I. Title.
  E382.V46 2004
  973.5'6'092—dc22

                                        2004000317

  2 3 4 5 6 7 8 9 10 R 14 13 12 11 10 09 08 07 06

Andrew Jackson was the seventh president of the United States. He was born in the Waxhaw region, an area along the border between North Carolina and South Carolina, in 1767. Jackson was one of the roughest, toughest presidents ever!

A painting showing a rural area in North Carolina in the early 1800s

Andrew Jackson was the first president to grow up poor and without an expensive education. The first six U.S. presidents all came from pretty wealthy families. All except George Washington were highly educated, too.

An engraving of a log cabin that may have been the birthplace of Andrew Jackson

The Waxhaw region, where Andrew grew up, was a rugged backwoods area. At that time, the Carolinas were part of thirteen colonies in North America that were ruled by Great Britain. Andrew lived in a log cabin with his mother and two brothers.

Andrew Jackson's father died just a few days before Andrew was born. Mrs. Jackson had to work very hard to raise her three sons alone. She hoped Andrew would become a minister someday. She saved every bit of extra money to send Andrew to the best school in the area.

Andrew didn't really care about school, though. He was a good reader but was more interested in running and jumping contests, horseback riding, hunting, and especially fighting. Worst of all, hot-tempered Andrew Jackson swore a lot!

The first battle of the Revolutionary War began in Lexington, Massachusetts, in 1775.

Andrew Jackson grew up during a very exciting time. In 1775, when Andrew was eight years old, the people of the American colonies began fighting the Revolutionary War, a war of independence against Great Britain and the King of England.

By the time British soldiers reached the Waxhaw region, Andrew was thirteen years old. Andrew and his two older brothers volunteered to join the American army right away.

This illustration shows a young Andrew Jackson watching the British attack the Waxhaw region.

During the fighting, Andrew and his brother, Robert, were captured by British soldiers. An officer who wanted his boots cleaned demanded that Andrew do the job. When Andrew refused, the British officer slashed him with his sword, leaving bad cuts on Andrew's hand and face.

This print, called "The Brave Boy of the Waxhaws," shows Andrew Jackson refusing to clean the boots of a British officer.

The British surrendered to General George Washington at Yorktown, Virginia, in 1781.

Andrew Jackson never forgot this.
He hated the British for the rest of his life.
The Revolutionary War was very tragic
for Andrew Jackson. By the time it ended,
both of his brothers and his mother had died.
At the age of fifteen, Andrew was both a
war veteran and an orphan.

Andrew Jackson spent his time as a teenager moving from relative to relative. He started hanging around with some bad kids who liked to drink, gamble, and play pranks on people. One of their favorite pranks was to dig up an outhouse and drag it to an unexpected place.

After a while, Andrew figured there must be something better he could do with his life. He decided to return to school. Andrew studied hard and even ended up teaching for a while.

A portrait of Rachel Donelson Jackson in 1826 (The Hermitage)

Eventually, Andrew became a lawyer. In 1788, when he was twenty-one years old, he headed west to make his fortune. Andrew thought he could help bring law and order to the untamed wilderness areas of Tennessee while helping settlers start up their new businesses. Andrew rented a room in the house of the Donelson family in Nashville, Tennessee.

The Donelsons were one of the richest families around. It wasn't long before Andrew fell in love with one of the Donelson daughters, Rachel. Rachel was beautiful and was a great horseback rider and singer. Rachel even smoked a corncob pipe!

In 1792, Andrew and Rachel got married. Andrew became a successful frontier lawyer. Because a lot of the people he helped didn't have money, he was often paid in cotton, whiskey, slaves, land, or farm animals. Andrew and Rachel were able to start up a large plantation. Backwoods settlers really appreciated Andrew's help and the fair way he treated them.

After a few years, Andrew was elected
to represent his state in Congress. He later
became a judge in the Superior Court of
Tennessee. Andrew Jackson ran his court in
a tough, no-nonsense way. He settled problems
quickly and usually kept a pistol or two
by his side. Because of his rugged frontier
upbringing, Andrew Jackson was used to
settling his problems with a gun.

Andrew Jackson's talent for fighting came in handy when the United States went to war with Britain again in 1812. For years, the British navy had been stopping American ships and kidnapping sailors for its own crews. At that same time, American settlers were beginning to move into areas where American Indians lived. The British started supplying some American Indians with weapons so they could force American settlers out of Indian territory.

In 1813, Andrew Jackson was asked to command an army of volunteers to defeat the Creek Indians. Even though Andrew had bullets left in him from a previous duel and a tavern fight, he and his men beat the Creek Indians badly.

A portrait of Davy Crockett

Two of Andrew's volunteer fighters were the famous frontiersmen Davy Crockett and Sam Houston.

A portrait of Sam Houston

After fighting the Creeks, Andrew Jackson led his troops to victory in what would become known as the Battle of New Orleans. Andrew knew he would be greatly outnumbered by British soldiers. He quickly gathered some of the best and most unusual fighters to help his army of volunteers. Former slaves, Creoles, backwoodsmen,

General Andrew Jackson (at left, on white horse) during the Battle of New Orleans

wealthy businessmen, Indians, and even pirates
all offered to help General Andrew Jackson.

Many of these volunteers were the best shots
around. By the time the fighting ended, the
British had lost almost two thousand men.
The Americans had lost only thirteen. Andrew
Jackson had won an almost impossible battle.
He suddenly became a national hero.

Because Andrew Jackson was such a courageous military leader and always looked out for the safety of his troops, his men nicknamed him Old Hickory. Hickory wood was the toughest living thing they knew of. It wasn't long before some people began to think Andrew Jackson would make a good president.

The sheet-music cover for a popular song written in Jackson's honor

A portrait by Ralph Earl of Andrew Jackson in military uniform on his horse

Andrew ran for president in 1824. He just missed winning the election against John Quincy Adams. Andrew and his supporters were furious. Andrew Jackson didn't like losing anything to anyone!

Andrew Jackson and his friends didn't waste a moment getting ready for the next election. In 1828, Andrew ran for president against John Quincy Adams again. It was a fierce battle. Both sides insulted the other's candidate. They said things that weren't always true and were often hurtful.

When the election was over, Andrew Jackson had won. Farmers, shop owners, settlers, and other everyday people felt they could trust Jackson because he was the first president to come from a poor frontier family. Andrew never forgot the common people who voted for him. He always tried to keep them in mind when he made his decisions.

Andrew Jackson had the support of everyday Americans such as the people shown here.

This illustration shows Andrew Jackson on his way to Washington, D.C., after winning the presidential election of 1828.

Unfortunately, just before Andrew began his new job as president, a terrible thing happened. His wife Rachel died. In 1829, a sad Andrew Jackson traveled to the White House alone. He ended up serving two four-year terms as president.

Supporters flocked to the White House on the day of President Jackson's inauguration in 1829.

Andrew Jackson was one of the most powerful leaders the United States ever had. During his time as president, Andrew made many important decisions. Some were very good, but some were pretty bad. One of the worst ones was supporting a law called the Indian Removal Act.

By the 1830s, thousands of Americans were moving west, settling the land and hoping to find a better life. A lot of this land, however, belonged to American Indians. Many settlers of the time viewed these Indians as being in the way—as well as dangerous. Andrew Jackson and other members of the government shared this viewpoint.

With President Jackson's support, Congress passed the Indian Removal Act. Its goal was

This painting by Valjean Hessing shows how thousands of Choctaw people were forced to leave their lands and walk hundreds of miles to Oklahoma. (Philbrook Museum of Art, Tulsa)

to move all Indians living east of the Mississippi River to lands west of the river. Eventually, the United States forced thousands of Creek, Choctaw, Blackhawk, Sauk, Seminole, and Cherokee from their lands, often after bloody battles. Not everyone supported the Indian Removal Act, but most people didn't seem to care about the cruel treatment of American Indians.

Andrew Jackson was never afraid to challenge anyone or anything that he felt might harm the United States. When he learned that the powerful Second National Bank of the United States was being run by just a few wealthy businessmen, he became angry. These men were able to control most of the money in the United States without any one watching over them. They could easily use public money for their own private gain.

Also, these bankers never helped poor working people who needed loans to start up new businesses and improve their farms. Andrew Jackson hated the Second National Bank so much he forced it to go out of business.

Once, when the state of South Carolina refused to go along with a national law, President Jackson really became angry. He said that states couldn't break laws decided by the U.S. government. If they began doing this, the country could fall apart. The president then said the United States would go to war with South Carolina if it didn't change its mind. Fortunately, a compromise was worked out and an early civil war was avoided.

A photograph of Andrew Jackson as an older man

Andrew Jackson was the first president to work hard for everyday people. He paved the way for people to take part in the U.S. government even if they weren't born wealthy and well-connected.

After he retired as president, Andrew Jackson spent time taking care of his plantation in Tennessee. He died there in 1845 at the age of seventy-eight.